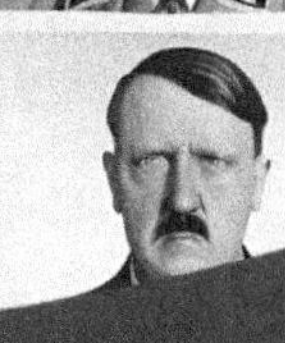

HITLER'S COHORTS

A Brief History of the People that Kept Him in Power

HISTORY ENCOUNTERS

Hitler's Cohorts

A Brief History of the People that Kept Him in Power

Contents

Preview Introduction

During his time Hitler seemed like a hero to the Germans. After the shame of the First World War and the Walmer Republic's fall, Hitler returned dignity to the German people. But in many of the narrations of his life and antics, it is often left out how he couldn't have achieved the success he did as a German dictator without the help and support of many people who, in their own right, were just as evil as him.

Chapter One: Introduction

When Hitler triumphed in the summer of 1940, it seemed like he was on the verge of winning the war. He had conquered Eastern Europe and gotten Poland even though his second-in-command had advised him against it. The effect was that there was intervention from Britain (personified by Winston Churchill). Hitler was becoming too ambitious and taking on more than he could chew. But was it more than he could chew? No one thought this seemingly quiet, unassuming man would eventually become the fuhrer. Until now, Hitler had defied all odds and proven that nothing was impossible for him. Or was it?

Hitler is often the poster child for the Holocaust and World War II, while almost every other name seems to fade into history books except for Winston Churchill, who put up a mighty front against Germany. In reality, Hitler did not do what he did by himself and couldn't have achieved the great acts of evil he managed without support from various sources that were just or even eviler than he was.

Hitler was not a man of war or strategy, but events eventually seemed to align in his favor. The infamous beer hall putsches he planned failed dismally, showing that he didn't know how to command a fighting unit. He didn't have the capabilities to win a battle, let alone a war, but it seemed that he was often aligned with highly talented people who propelled him forward. Hitler's greatest strengths were manipulation and talking. He had to be a snake-oil salesman because he was selling the Germans their darkest dream. In order to sell that snake oil, he needed someone who would carry his message far and wide and who also had a deep hatred for the Jews, which he had in Joseph Goebbels. Goebbels was said to hate Jews more than Hitler and ensured that antisemitic propaganda was anywhere and everywhere.

Hitler was not a man of war, so to avoid further embarrassments such as the beer hall putsches, he needed people who were strong in warfare, which he found in Heinrich Himmler and less so in Hermann Göring. Hitler talked about exterminating the Jews, but Himmler eventually created the concentration camps for Hitler's approval. They committed many acts of murder and executed the groundwork that laid the solid foundation for Nazi rule.

The bigwigs were nothing at the end of the day without the cooperation of the German everyday people. Many want to blame the actions of the Germans on their leaders, but inevitably human choice is a real factor. The general German republic hated the Jews. It was only a minority that tried to stand up for what was right and humane against the Nazis. Those people were reported on and sold out by other Germans, leading to their executions or fleeing to other countries to avoid supporting the Nazis. The general public sold out people they had grown up with, done business with, and performed with. The general public supported the Nazis burning of all Jewish literature. The general public then tried to blame all their actions on Hitler when it was evident that many of the atrocities had been of their own evil volition.

In that sense, it behooves us all that history will always have its major villain, but the villain rarely, if ever, worked alone. Hitler certainly did not.

Chapter Two: How Ordinary People Became Nazis

How Ordinary People Became Nazis, Hitler interacting with his supporters at the height of his success

With the end of the First World War, the German people were desperate. Suffering from hyperinflation and hunger, they wanted some kindness and hope. The Allied powers of the First World War had won and wanted to get as many reparations as possible and also punish the Germans for the damages caused by the war leading to the collapse of the German economy. That lack of empathy and compassion would have consequences that they would never have predicted.

The Allied Powers were right to be angry with the Germans. During the war, their own people had suffered, millions had died, and their resources had been drained. But when it comes to wars, it's not as black and white as one country is right or wrong. Because inevitably, countries are made up of people who didn't consent to be citizens and were just born into it.

After Germany realized the First World War was unwinnable and agreed to sign an armistice in 1918 to end the fighting. With the end of the empirical rule, there were riots all over the nation and the threat of a communist takeover. Major political parties joined in order to suppress the uprising establishing the Weimar Republic. The Weimar Republic had the awful task of completing the treaty's conditions, which saw Germany losing a lot of territories, taking full responsibility for the war, and paying debilitating reparations on an already weakened economy. The nationalist Germans were enraged by this because they staunchly believed that the war could have been won if politicians and protestors had not betrayed their army.

This is what would fuel Hitler's ideologies. Later on, he would use that mindset to pin all the woes that the Germans had gone through on Jews. At that time, Germany was filled with many Anti-Semitic people even though many Jews had integrated into German society. The Germans continued to see them as outsiders. After World War I, Jewish success led to unfounded accusations of profiteering and laundering. Many conspiracy theories were created out of fear, anger, and bigotry.When Hitler joined a small nationalist party, the people were receptive to his message, and he quickly rose in rank. The tide of ill will against the Jews empowers the Nazis to denounce communism and capitalism.The Nazi party was not popular at the time. After an attempt to overthrow the government, the party was banned, and Hitler was jailed for treason.

Upon his release a year later, he immediately began to rebuild the movement. In 1929, the Great Depression happened, which led to America withdrawing its loans from Germany. Germany's economy crumbled at the speed of light in a way the republic could not have planned for. Hunger and desperation made the general public rapid for an answer to their problems. Most parties proved incompetent at handling the crisis, while the opposition was too fragmented by internal struggles. The people were frustrated and angry. The Nazis, with their over-confidence and their ability to shift the blame for everything on Jews, gave them the best answer to their issues which saw the political group's support in parliamentary votes go from a measly 3% all the way to 18% in a span of two years. In 1932, Hitler ran for president, losing the election to war hero General von Hindenburg. But with 36% of the vote, Hitler demonstrated the extent of his support.

Von Hindenburg's advisors told him it would be wise to appoint Hitler as Chancellor to channel his popularity for their goals. Though the chancellor was only the administrative hand of the parliament, Hitler made sure that he could do more than his role legally required and formed several paramilitary groups.

Hitler soon raised fears of a communist uprising. He convinced the Germans that only he could restore law and order.A young worker was found guilty of setting the parliament building on fire in 1933. Hitler used the incident as leverage to obtain emergency powers from the government. The freedom of the press was eliminated, further parties were dissolved, and anti-Jewish laws were implemented in a couple of months. Along with potential rivals, many of Hitler's early radical supporters were detained and put to death. It was obvious when President Hindenburg passed away in August 1934 that there would be no new election. Hitler's meteoric rise to power didn't require mass repression, he just used his speeches to convince people that his way was best for exploring people's fears and ire. This was effective enough to drive majority support to the Nazis. The privileged classes, which included academics and entrepreneurs, chose the side most beneficial to them and endorsed Hitler. They convinced themselves and each other that his more extreme rhetoric was only for show.

The ordinary people became Nazis overnight, showing that democracy is weak amongst angry, hungry crowds desperate for a solution.

Chapter Three: The Role of von Hindenburg in Empowering Hitler

The role of von Hindenburg in empowering Hitler, Paul von Hindenburg in front of a portrait of himself

It is interesting to note that possibly the biggest contribution to Hitler's rise in power and an unintentional cohort was a man against his policies and belief system. Paul von Hindenburg was a celebrated war hero. He gained notoriety during World War I. He came from an aristocratic family and generally grew up in prestige and privilege. Despite that, he was a disciplined and hardworking man and fought in the Austro-Prussian war of 1866 and the Franco-Prussian war of 1870-1871. His feats in the war won him many accolades, and he was a symbol of German pride.

Hindenburg was extremely successful as a man of war and often orchestrated the defeat of many of Germany's enemies through tact and intelligence. The first time he would be called out of retirement would be during the First World War. He worked along with General Erich Ludendorff to reverse the damage that had been done and stop a very embarrassing defeat for the German army. Once Hindenburg stepped into the war, the Russians were defeated at the battle of Tannenberg. This win was also critical in the eventual capitulation of the entire Russian force during the war. He managed to get the eastern side of the war under German control and instilled rules to bring "civilization" to the other European societies. When the Germans lost the war on the Western front, von Hindenburg was called in to intervene, hoping he could work his magic there. Unfortunately, the war was too far gone for even Hindenburg to save.

Von Hindenburg believed that the German army had been stabbed in the back by liberals. This is evidenced by what he said when he was sent to testify about the German loss during the war. He believed that the Germans had not really lost the war. Probably his strong sense of pride and identity were hurt by the loss of the Germans during the war. After the war, he went into his second retirement.

Von Hindenburg had the people's trust, and they viewed him

as a symbol of the former pride of Germany. As the Weimar Republic failed and there was political disunity in the country, the people turned back to the symbol of Germany's former pride for guidance. Von Hindenburg was encouraged to enter politics for the first time. This would also be the first time that Hitler would run for president. It was a battle between the old German pride and a man that promised Germany a brighter future and new glory. Von Hindenburg won the election, but it was clear that Hitler had the support of the younger generation unfamiliar with von Hindenburg's feats. With advice from people around him, he decided to try and utilize Hitler's popularity for his own benefit. They thought that it would ensure the support of the Nazis and, in turn, stabilize the government.

It can be said that perhaps von Hindenburg was of advanced age and wasn't in the greatest mental capacity when he became president, which is why he underestimated Hitler. By making Hitler chancellor and giving the Nazis two seats in parliament, he thought he could infiltrate the Nazis and take control from behind the scenes. It can be said that it's likely that von Hindenburg was tired and didn't have the same drive as when he was younger. He was being forced out of retirement for a second time and entering a field he had never worked in before. Von Hindenburg and his advisors grossly underestimated Hitler. Hitler seemed non-threatening, but he was very calculating and could influence people. It can be said that Hitler was an example of the first "influencer."

Von Hindenburg was also highly influenced by his advisor and confidant, Major General von Schleicher, who wanted a government free of parliamentary intervention. He was all in favor of an authoritarian rule. It is thought that it is because of the influence of von Schleicher that von Hindenburg allowed Hitler to be chancellor. Von Hindenburg, systematically moving power away from the government and dissolving the Reichstag, laid the foundation for Hitler to take full control of Germany. One of the vital things von Hindenburg established was that any government decision could be overthrown with the president's veto.

As he grew older, it could be seen that Hindenburg was growing tired. He didn't have the energy to take action and supported Hitler's increasingly outrageous feats. Perhaps he never thought that Hitler would ever be the threat that the former chancellor had been who had tried to thwart von Hindenburg openly. But the greatest thing that he possibly did to aid and empower Hitler was to die, leaving Hitler with complete control over Germany.

The role of von Hindenburg in empowering Hitler, von Hindenburg's memorial

Chapter Four: Nazism Around the World and How They Supported Hitler

Young Nazi soldiers in front of a tank

The sentiments that the Nazis held towards Jews were not isolated to only them or just Germany. Considering that in every country they went into, they could garner support for their cause of exterminating Jews except in a few places (ironically, one of the people that didn't support the Nazi tyranny against Jews was Benito Mussolini. Although he never outrightly opposed Hitler, there have been reports that Nazis got very little support from Italians against Jews and that the concentration camps in Italy, though still inhumane, were much better than those found elsewhere. What some people have panned as "Hitlerism" was not only limited to Hitler, and many erase from history the groups of people who contributed to Nazicism even though they were from the allied countries.

An example is that Nazis had a very strong hold in America during the time of Hitler. Millions of Americans of German origin were sympathetic to the views and systems of their motherland during the presidential run of Franklin D. Roosevelt. They would make camps (which were publicly known) where they would train for the time that the Führer would need their services during the war. It's highly likely that this group of people also worked as spies for Germany during the height of the war. Sinclair Lewis, who won an internationally recognized award in literature, made it clear that fascism could easily get a stronghold in America. Many Americans hated the idea that they were supporting the British and the Allies during the war. America itself was prejudiced against many groups of people, including Jews. Lewis stated that fascism in America would take the face of freedom of speech away, incarcerate political opponents and use violence in the guise of law to "keep order" in the country (which is what inevitably happened to Germany under Hitler).

In fact, many of the Americans who believed in isolationism at first believed the tactics of Hitler were admirable and that he was taking back the land of the Germans from usurpers. White supremacy and the theory of there being an Aryan race matched quite well, considering during that time, America had its own prejudices; it seemed Germany was taking actions America was not yet ready to implement fully. Hitler's diplomats in America handed out and spread as much propaganda as possible, especially among people they knew were of Germanic origin. Many people state that the war got as bad as it did because Roosevelt (and, in turn, America) remained apathetic for a very long time towards the plight of Jews in America and the concentration camps that were formed there.

America isn't the only country that would like to erase its not-so-stellar compliance with Hitler. The French government and people needed someone to blame when France fell into Germany's hands during the Blitzkrieg (when the Nazis took control of the North of France and over five thousand of their soldiers). And the blame inexplicably fell on the Jews showing that anti-Semiticism was not germane to only the Germans. The Jews had been facing animosity for decades before the invasion. It seemed that the German invasion became an excuse for the French to show their hidden vitriol to the Jews and eliminate their own Jewish problem. The Jews that had escaped Germany found themselves betrayed in France and shipped off to concentration camps, camps were made in France. Jews' houses were repossessed, and thousands were killed in the gas chambers. This was part of France's way of returning to a more conservative life.

Some argue that the Vichy government (which ruled France then) was in a tight position and only participated in anti-

Semitism for self-preservation. Still, in actuality, anti-Jewish laws were already being implemented before any invasion had taken place. They had already prohibited Jews from being in public service or owning property. The French public supported these actions taken openly, and Jews were deported to concentration camps. In modern-day France, it's taken the people a long time to acknowledge that even though they are considered on the "hero" side of winning World War II, they are not, in essence, heroes, and their predecessors aided Hitler. It wasn't until 1995 that then-President Jacques Chirac acknowledged France's role in the death of hundreds of thousands of Jews.

Hitler was on a manhunt to exterminate every Jew that he could, and he revealed that in every country that Germany managed to invade, there was enough unjust stigma against one group of people to push them to do things that were truly inhumane.

Chapter Five: Joseph Goebbels

Many people know Joseph Goebbels as the man that was meant to rule after Hitler. There were many uncanny similarities between Goebbels and Hitler. They both were known to be powerful orators and extremely anti-Semitic (Goebbels was said to hate Jews more than Hitler). At first, they both wanted to infiltrate the arts industry and somehow pursued politics (Hitler wanted to be an artist and Goebbels a writer). Hitler became the booster child for the Nazis, but it can be said that Goebbels was just as bad. Goebbels controlled all the Nazi propaganda and made sure that he influenced how Germans thought through the media (specifically radio).

Goebbels carefully orchestrated campaigns that secured widespread support for the Nazis and ensured that the Jews were viewed as enemies. Radio was something that wasn't widespread in Germany before Goebbels's time. Still, he ensured that most German households had small radios to listen to Nazi propaganda. The people astounded by this new technology were programmed to think a certain way by constant Nazi broadcasting and listening to Hitler's speeches. The same radio device also served to help save the lives of many of the marginalized communities (Jews and others) because they would be able to know what the Nazis' next moves were.

The irony of Goebbels being such an evil figure was that physically he was not threatening, much like Hitler himself. He was only about five feet tall and walked limply from having a club foot. He was as far as you could get from the ideal Aryan image that both he and Hitler promoted (which, ironically, neither fit). The Nazis also euthanized those with disabilities during their reign, saying that disabled people tainted Syrian blood, while the man that terrorized and ruled Berlin under Nazi rule was disabled.

If anyone noticed the disparity between the message Goebbels spread through Hitler and his own being, they were probably too scared to mention it. Criticism of the Nazi party's main leadership meant death or concentration camp (another form of death). Goebbels understood that if one could control the information people had access to, he could control the people. That's why one of the first things he did when Hitler came into power was to have a big event where the Nazi youth burned all books in the vicinity that Jewish authors wrote. During this event, Goebbels spoke about how "the era of exaggerated Jewish intellectualism is over. The breakthrough of the German revolution has also once again cleared the path for the German way," Over 25,000 volumes of books were burnt during that event. He could trick the Germans into believing that what they were doing was strengthening German pride. Goebbels didn't end there. He ordered that videos of the event be played in cinemas across the country. His goal, from the get-go, was to turn the nation of Germany against Jews. His media control had to be absolute because the more extreme a movement is, the more propaganda one needs in order to garner support.

When it was clear that the Nazis were losing and Hilter committed suicide at the end of World War II, Goebbels killed himself the day after, on 1 May 1945. He knew that he could never outlive the atrocities that they had committed.

Chapter Six: Heinrich Himmler

Heinrich Himmler as a child

Heinrich Himmler was one of the main architects of the Nazi Holocaust. Being the middle-class son of a schoolteacher, he would become the driving force between German attempting to create a master race and attempting the genocide of millions. The scariest thing about Himmler is that he seemed to have an idealistic childhood, and nothing could have set him up to become an architect of terror in the Nazi regime eventually. Some people speculate, though, that his rocky relationship with his father may have been the thing that would have led him to seek that male validation through radicalism.

Himmler allegedly became radicalized in Munich when he was only nineteen. He had been too young to fight in the First World War but old enough to understand the full effects of losing. Himmler would frequent beer halls where predominantly men would sit together, socialize, and share political thoughts. In 1929, Himmler would hear Hitler railing on about the Jews across the beer halls of Munich. During the German crisis after World War I, it became quite common to blame the Jews for the country's state. They blamed the Jews for being loyal only to each other and their international interests. One of the common mentalities was that Jews would hide finance so that they wouldn't have to support Germany when the country needed aid. It can also be deduced Himmler was at a stage in his life where he was trying to figure out his identity and was easily influenced. He became popular among the fascists in the bar because he was a good dancer.

Himmler had had a fascination with war from a young age. One of the defining moments of his youth was that he could not participate in World War I and felt jealous that his older brother had been of age to serve. He wanted to prove his worth as well. This eagerness eventually led him to sign up for the Nazi party in 1923. He would take part in Hilter's first attempt to overthrow the democratic government during the 1923 beer hall putsch. Himmler felt that this was the time to prove his worth as a soldier.

While Hitler was jailed for the coup, Himmler used that time to grow in the ranks of the Nazi party. Himmler emerged unscathed from the coup because, according to the judicial system, there wasn't enough evidence to implicate him. He was able to move up so quickly because many of the major Nazi leaders were arrested during the beer hall putsches leading to many opportunities for growth. By 1927 he had become the leader of the *SS*, which would originally start off as Hitler's bodyguard. He would spread antisemitic conspiracies to expand the image of a perfect Aryan race unblemished by "inferior" blood.

He promoted *lebensborn,* a program to promote the Aryan population. He made sure that German women were screened to ensure they were pure-blooded enough. He wanted to increase the Germanic population to 120 million. Only about 40% of women met Himmler's racial purity criteria. Families who were Aryan were instructed to have a minimum of four children each.

Hitler recognized his passion for racial purity from Himmler, and during the Nazi invasion of Poland, he appointed Himmler Reich Commissar to strengthen the German Ethnic Stock. This gave Himmler the power to determine who could be considered German and where Germans could live. basically had control over the German identity. Himmler made plans for where the increased German population would settle down, creating a program to move non-Aryan people from those lands. Nazi soldiers were encouraged to reproduce, so many illegitimate children were sired. This goal was aided by the *Einsatzgruppen,* a mobile killing unit that got rid of all undesirables, namely Jews, people with disabilities, the Roma, and anyone else who did not have the favor of the Nazis. The need for mass shootings and murders to fulfill his goal as Germany invaded Russia and other territories would increase to Himmler creating concentration camps to handle the load. The creation of concentration camps greatly impressed Hitler and led him to green-light the creation of more camps.

By the war's end, Himmler tried to escape and hide but was eventually caught by the allied forces. He had used a false identity to travel with other former SS soldiers. When interrogated and asked for identification, the stamp on his identity document revealed that many SS officers used it to avoid detection. Before they could do anything to him, he ate a pill containing cyanide and died within fifteen minutes despite attempts to revive him on 25 May 1945.

Chapter Seven: Hermann Göring

Hermann Göring was Hitler's second-in-command. Born into a distinguished family, he was charming, flamboyant, and a ruthless manipulator. Göring was addicted to wealth and power and willing to obtain it by any means necessary. He was known to be a boisterous man who didn't care who he shackled up with as long as he could enjoy the benefits. He ate like a horse and loved luxury and power. It's also suspected that he had a drug problem. Göring might have been the most colorful character out of all of Hitler's cohorts. He didn't fit the stoic/ no-nonsense image of the ideal German man.

The difference between Göring and the other Nazi leaders is that he had served in the First World War and received accolades for his skills as a pilot fighter. If he had not joined the Nazis, he would have gone down in history as a dashing man of action and war hero. Göring exhibited all the traits of a psychopath or, at the very least, a narcissist. He was cunning, manipulative, charming, and had a certain level of cruelty that made him open to Nazi idealism.

During the First World War, Göring had first enlisted in the infantry but quickly realized that the greatest accolades were given to pilots who operated in the skies, so he quickly became part of the Air Force. Göring flew a Fokker D7. It was the most advanced plane of its day and far superior to what the allies had. It had a top speed of 187 km/hr. The pilots were known as knights in the sky. Göring managed to shoot down 22 enemy aircraft. During this time in his life, he earned the Iron Cross 1st Class honor, Iron Cross 2nd Class honor, a Blood Order honor, King Cross of the Iron Class, Grand Cross of the Iron Class, Golden Party Badge, and the Pour le Mérite. Someone who got these honors was considered the rockstar of that day. But then GöringMs glorious time came to an abrupt stop with the sudden surrender of the German army. He felt that Germany had been stabbed in the back. He also deeply resented the terms that the allies had imposed on Germany. He started to look for radical solutions and found them in Nazism.

Göring met Hitler in the heart of Munich, where Hitler was proselytizing for the Nazi regime. He would go on to join the party and start a meteoric rise in the Nazi regime. The relationship between Hitler and Göring was one of the most destructive the world has ever seen. They would work together to try and overthrow the Bavarian government and establish a Nazi government. Göring would be mortally wounded during the putsch and shot in the groin. His supporters managed to sneak him away and deal with his gun wound. They gave him morphine to deal with the pain, which would be the beginning of his morphine addiction. Due to being wanted, Göring had to flee to Sweden. His mental state deteriorated greatly during that time, becoming a violent addict. He had to be confined in a straitjacket but managed to kick the habit or perhaps not show his addiction so openly. He would return to Germany in 1927 when amnesty was declared. Göring would slowly work his way up in politics again and eventually be one of the few Nazis to gain a seat in the *Reichstag*. Hitler began to see him as the Nazi public relations officer for outsiders.

Göring established the Gestapo in 1933. Under Göring, the Gestapo was instructed to "shoot first and inquire afterward, and if you make mistakes, I will protect you". He was a killer and murderer, willing to do anything for Hitler. But in 1939, when Hitler wanted to invade Poland, Göring tried to talk him out of the plan. He was against Germany starting a Second World War. Another world war might mean that Göring would lose everything he had gained as a Nazi. Göring had collected a smorgasbord of titles, including President of the Reichstag, Reich Minister of Aviation, Commander in Chief of the Luftwaffe, Reich Minister of Economics, General Field Marshal, and Marshal of the Reich. He collected titles like collectibles. That much power was not sustainable.

When the Nazis eventually lost the war, Göring heard that Hitler was about to commit suicide. When Göring heard that, he sent Hitler a telegram asking if that meant he could assume control of the Reich. Hitler interpreted that as betrayal, stripped him of all his titles and position in the party, and ordered his arrest. Despite his fallout with Hitler, Göring was still charged at the Nuremberg trials. He was found guilty of multiple things, including crimes against humanity. He committed suicide before they could kill him by hanging.

Chapter Eight: The Common Cohorts: Why the Germans Didn't Resist Hitler

German concentration camp

There is a popular analogy about a frog in hot water. If you throw the frog in a pot of boiling water, it will jump out immediately. But if you put a frog in a pot of cold water on a stove and increase the heat slowly, it will boil to death. The Nazis didn't take complete control and mass murdered people immediately. They at first seemed like a non-threatening party full of hot air and overly energetic youth. Hitler was not a physically imposing man whom the leaders had to be wary of. Traditionally, men had to be fighters of great prestige and from certain backgrounds to enact major changes. Hitler just talked a lot. They would later realize that words can be more powerful than swords. It also proved that the country was democratic until the financial depression.

Hitler could not have retained power if not for the common German people. The soldiers listened to their leaders' directions. Workers from all walks of life supported the creation of an Aryan race. But the atrocities committed by the Nazis were, perhaps, in the end, a result of fear of punishment had they decided not to follow the leadership rather than an actual belief in their system.

The Germans hated the presence of Jews, but many stated that they were unaware of the conditions that the Jews were put through in concentration camps. That view should be taken with a grain of salt, though, as it was widely known that people who were part of undesirable groups were killed mercilessly. When people at the concentration camps were finally freed, many soldiers who had been through many wars were still in shock over the conditions the Jews were kept in. Even though this was under the command of Heinrich Himmler, many of the German soldiers still carried out their orders. That's why at the end of the world war, many committed suicides; they didn't want to face the possibility of being treated the same way they had treated other people.

In modern times, people who worked for the Nazi regime

are still being held accountable for their crimes. The most recent case was in 2022 of a 101-year-old man sentenced to five years in prison because of his role as a Nazi guard during the Holocaust serving at Sachsenhausen concentration camp. In 2021 Irmgard F., at the age of 97, was taken to court to face trial for her crimes against humanity, having worked as a secretary of the SS commander in Stutthof concentration camp. The similarities with these cases are that the people tried to lie that they had nothing to do with the Nazi regime during their time and were innocent bystanders/citizens. But it's known that during the Holocaust, even your neighbor would sell you out and have you taken to Auschwitz, as evidenced by the story of Anne Frank.

At the end of the day, the general public couldn't claim that it was the Nazis that made them do it because they were the ones that put Hitler in power in the first place of their prejudices against Jewish people.

Chapter Nine: Hitler, the Scapegoat

Wax Figures of Hitler and Churchill

Adolf Hitler himself was not a physically imposing man, as many have mentioned. If one critiques his looks according to modern-day criteria, one can even say he looks like a nerd. So how did someone who couldn't pass the criteria for being Aryan himself manage to trick people into believing he was a strong leader? It was obvious from the word "go" that Hitler was devious, a liar, and a manipulator. The fact that he killed and imprisoned many of the people that had helped him rise to power in the first place showed that he didn't stand for something in particular but was using a belief system that would get him into power, much like Gröning. Many historians have pointed out that Hitler has become a convenient scapegoat to mask the multiple atrocities of many people who are rarely spoken about. Being the leader and the face of the movement, Hitler would garner more attention, and the greatest punishment was earned him. But many of his followers want to evade punishment and blame by putting the blame on him.

The greatest example of someone who worked with Hitler and tried to escape punishment is Gröning. When the Nuremberg trials were conducted, he was seen laughing and poking fun at his accusers. In retrospect, he may have been trying to portray the image of someone who was too lackadaisical and ignorant to be aware of the war crimes. When presented with images of what was happening at the concentration camps, Gröning pretended to be shocked and lied that he was unaware of how terrible the camps were. The court proved that Gröning was aware of when enemy soldiers were brutally killed and had visited a concentration camp before, so he did know what was happening. Gröning had tried to pass the blame onto Himmler and also Hitler.

That's a recurring trend in those that worked on the side of the Nazis during World War II. The argument brought forth by many is that if Hitler was such a strong and great evil man, why did he commit suicide when he knew that he was going to lose? When the Germans lost the First World War, the aristocracy was stripped of its power, and Emperor Wilhelm II was disgraced.

He spent the rest of his life in exile in the Netherlands. He made terrible decisions that caused a terrible war, but no one could accuse him of being a coward. Hitler, on the other hand, chose to commit suicide than face things, showing that despite his promotion of strong Aryan men, he was, in fact, a coward. Hitler even wanted to appoint Gröning as his successor when Gröning had proven incompetent and unreliable multiple times. Hitler was obviously inefficient, but the joint extremist feelings against Jews and other non-Germans created a system that everyone contributed to but was completely blamed on one man because no one wanted to face the consequences of their actions. At the end of the day, they all knew what they had done was terrible and inexcusable, but they had lived in a bubble where there would be German supremacy because of their own greed. Hitler, on many occasions, proved he was a coward. And the tide of anti-Semiticism used a coward to come to fruition. Hitler wasn't even there to defend himself as various war criminals, and his collaborators tried to pin the entire blame on him.

Chapter Ten: Modern-Day Neo-Nazis

A Nazi propaganda poster with antisemitic content

There is a growing belief system that history should never be censored or watered down so that we know the full extent of how deprived humans can be. Humans have a tendency to repeat patterns of the past. A former shopkeeper mentioned that items that flew off the shelf the fastest in modern-day Germany were anything with Nazi insignia. Previously it was unacceptable and taboo to make jokes about World War II and Nazism, but in the present day, those jokes have suddenly become acceptable again. Does it signal a danger of another movement that could result in the same devastating effects of World War II? Tamar Dreifuss (a Holocaust survivor) states that oftentimes it is not enough just to remember but to take action consistently to avoid repeating the mistakes of the past.

Neo-Nazis strive to reinstate Nazi ideology and believe that the Nazis were betrayed during World War II, much like the people of the Weimar Republic after World War I. Neo Nazis also tie in with White Supremacy because of their versions of the ideal human match. Blonde hair, blue eyes, and of Anglo-Saxon, Scandinavian, Nordic, or Germanic origin. They promote the separation of people of different races. The only point where they differ is that Nazis staunchly believe that Jews threaten the Aryan race and rank the lowest human existence, while White Supremacists often rank black people as the lowest. The Nazis would, in the past, determine the racial makeup of someone by examining their hair and facial features to determine their Aryan purity. They had a chart that they used as a reference to know how to classify people quickly, similar to the comb method used during apartheid and colonization in Africa to determine what race a person was to be classified as.

Their hatred towards Jews is still there but has also spread to include Muslims, whose population has grown in Germany during the time of Angela Merkel, who opened the borders to immigrants. The Neo-Nazis believe in the Nazi ideology of "Blood and Soil," which means that the Aryan race is superior and that the German people have a special connection to their land. They should only occupy it. Anyone who did not fit into the ideal German image was considered an "alien," "parasite," or a "degenerate." Dehumanizing non-Germanic groups was a tool to easily get people to commit acts of violence. Because it's easier to get people to do terrible things against people they consider different or less human than them.

Violence is still a threat to non-Germanic people in Germany. In 2020, a Jewish student was attacked with a shovel in a murder attempt in Hamburg. The student was repeatedly beaten over the head when trying to enter the synagogue. Other instances have happened where men wearing skull caps are often the targets of harassment and antisemitic attacks. On an international scale, American rapper Ye claimed that Hitler was right for trying to exterminate the Jews. Neo-Nazi/Nazi beliefs are moving to groups out of Germany. Fortunately, many organizations and anti-terrorist groups have been made aware of this. They are doing their best to limit the activities of these groups of people to avoid World War III.

Discussion Questions 1

Hitler is the poster child for World War II and the Holocaust. After finding out about the people that worked with him to bring his evil regime into place, do you feel like the blame is not equally split? That Hitler is a cover for the faults of his cohorts and the general German population that carried out his will during that time?

Discussion Questions 2

Do you believe that Germany could descend into such extremism today? It can be noted that when economic situations turn back, morality often goes out the window, as evidenced by increased crime worldwide during the Covid-19 pandemic when many lost their jobs. It can also be noted that the Germans proved more susceptible to Hitler's teaching when Germany's economy was down. Explain your answer.

Discussion Questions 3

People who worked or aided the Nazi regime are still being arrested today, with some war criminals being well into their 90s. Do you think this is necessary? Or pointless?

Discussion Questions 4

Which cohorts do you think had the most impact on the Nazi regime? Was it the Nazi leaders or the general public? Do you think that getting the general public not to trust and report on each other can maintain a dictatorship in a country?

Discussion Questions 5

Göring's daughter went through trials with her mother and got arrested. She spent the rest of her life a Nazi supporter and eventually a spy. Do you think people who benefited and were deeply in a prejudiced system can ever emancipate themselves from it?

Discussion Questions 6

Himmler created concentration camps, Goebbels promoted Nazi propaganda, and Gröning caused the senseless deaths of millions of people for his own wealth and benefit. Which of these top cohorts do you think was the worst? Why?

Discussion Questions 7

Why do you think people allow a belief system that they don't agree with to prevail? Hitler was able to rise to power even though many people disagreed with his ideologies. Did they truly think he was harmless or subconsciously agree with his ideologies? Explain your reasoning.

Discussion Questions 8

Do you think Hitler truly believed in the superiority of the Germans or was he an art reject that gained some notoriety speaking out against the Jews? The Aryan state that Hitler wanted to create inevitably seemed like a fairytale manufactured in his head that gave him power and consequence. Do you think this is a correct analysis of Hitler?

True or False Questions

1. The death of von Hindenburg was a leading factor in Hitler gaining full control of Germany. It's not certain if Nazism could have been curbed if von Hindenburg had lived, but perhaps their ascent wouldn't have been so pronounced.

2. Hitler utilized the hatred of the Jews in much of the German population in order to gain power. It was already too late when the Germans realized that Hitler wasn't benefiting them as a dictator.

3. Antisemitism has not ended in modern-day Germany, and many Neo-Nazi groups have sprouted up. Some are concentrating their hate on the rising number of Muslims in the country rather than Jews.

4. Hitler is often credited for all the atrocities to the point that

many other equally guilty parties are never mentioned. Joseph Goebbels is more responsible for the genocide of Jews because he created concentration camps and permitted mass murders of non-Aryan groups.

5. Hitler was tried during the Nuremberg trials for gross acts of inhumanity and other charges. He was sentenced to death by gunshot on 25 May 1946.

6. Hitler and his closest men all committed suicide inevitably. Many people interpret that as cowardly. If they had really believed in their regime, they would have stood trial and faced the consequences of their actions. But the Nazi leaders had shown on more than one occasion that they were not men who had a strong sense of purpose but just wanted power.

7. Göring's correspondence with Hitler when he heard that Hitler wanted to commit suicide in Berlin was intercepted and misconstrued to make it sound as though Göring wanted to take over power from Hitler. Leading to the downfall of Göring.

8. Hitler was a strong solution for the German people and had their best interests at heart. His methods were misinterpreted throughout history.

True or False Answer

1. *True.*
2. *True.*
3. *True.*
4. *False. Heinrich Himmler created the concentration camps and approved mass murders of people.*
5. *False. Hitler committed suicide before they could catch him.*
6. *True.*
7. *True.*
8. *False. Hitler didn't care about the German people or even the Nazis. He was power-hungry and overconfident.*

Conclusion

The world has progressed to a point where we no longer see the purpose of war. As evidenced by the reaction of many people when war goes on in the world. History needs to be learned so that we know and take consistent action to avoid the same mistakes as an addict in remission. Science has proven through epigenetics that personality traits and characteristics can be passed from one generation to the next through epigenomes. That could possibly mean that antisemitism, racism, and prejudice can be passed on if we are not constantly aware of our actions and where they stem from.

The existence of Neo-Nazis not fully versed in the history of World War II and the Holocaust is proof that history likes to repeat itself. The irony that they believe and follow the same foolish rhetoric that the Nazis fooled the German population with for the first time shows that humans don't usually try to research outside of their sphere of knowledge.

That prejudices always emerge in times of trouble, as the tide of crime, antisemitism, racism, and other prejudices have risen since the economic downturn caused by the Covid-19 pandemic.

Hans Frank, a Nazi leader's son who does not subscribe to the Nazi rhetoric though remains a proud German, claimed in an interview with BBC stated, "Don't trust us." Financial crises give extremists a strong foundation to enact great acts of terror and cruelty. That's why many dictators (an example is Kim Jong Un of North Korea) make sure that their people live below the poverty line to maintain control.

At the end of the day, the story of Hitler's cohorts is a lesson that we are all capable of great evil and good, even in the toughest situations. For sure, there were those Germans stuck so deep in the regime and were scared to lose their lives and everything they had if they showed opposition. But even in the darkness, at least one inspirational story shows that humans are capable of great acts of bravery.

Karl Plagge was a German army general. He saw that the SS were hellbent on killing all the Jews and devised a plan to save their lives. He risked his life running a covert operation and lying to his fellow Germans in order to do what was right. Even though many Jews were executed and buried in mass graves, Plagge saved as many as he could by digging places in the wall and ground where he could hide the escaped Jews until he could smuggle them to safety. In the grand scheme of things, it seemed like Plagge's efforts were useless.

Bibliography (Works Cited)

1. Free Documentary, Hitler's Henchmen: Episode 3. YouTube, <https://youtu.be/01WYa_XTOW4>
2. Free Documentary, Hitler's Henchmen Episode 1. YouTube, <https://youtu.be/ULIQRf-trdo>
3. Free Documentary, Hitler's Henchmen Episode 2. YouTube, <https://youtu.be/b9ASsVHa3ng>
4. Yad Vashem, Liberators and Survivors: The First Moments. YouTube, <https://youtu.be/kOIHRQlQqwU>
5. The Infographics Show, Why Didn't More Germans Resist Hitler's Regime. YouTube <https://youtu.be/kOIHRQlQqwU>
6. Wikipedia, Hermann Göring. Wikipedia <https://en.m.wikipedia.org/wiki/Hermann_Göring>
7. The National WWII Museum. An Architect of Terror: Heinrich Himmler and the Holocaust. The National WWII Museum New Orleans <https://www.nationalww2museum.org/war/articles/heinrich-himmler-holocaust>

Images (License-Free)

Part 1 How Ordinary People Became Nazis, Hitler interacting with his supporters at the height of his success. <https://commons.wikimedia.org/w/index.php?curid=5369386>

Part 1 The role of von Hindenburg in empowering Hitler, Paul von Hindenburg in front of a portrait of himself

<https://commons.wikimedia.org/w/index.php?curid=5370811>

Part 1 The role of von Hindenburg in empowering Hitler,

von Hindenburg's memorial <https://commons.wikimed ia.org/w/index.php?curid=5370811>

Part 2 Young Nazi soldiers in front of a tank <https://ww w.flickr.com/photos/96937621@N00/36553545530>

Part 2 A Nazi propaganda poster with antisemitic content
<https://www.flickr.com/photos/98676224@N00/76934

548>

**Part 3 Wax Figures of Hitler and Churchill + <https://ww
w.flickr.com/photos/25468903@N00/1289920278>**

Part 3 German concentration camp <https://unsplash.co m/photos/odeopNXzGNk>

Part 2 Heinrich Himmler as a child <https://commons.m
.wikimedia.org/wiki/File:Heinrich_Himmler_as_a_chil
d.jpg#mw-jump-to-license>